T0369358

WHAT'S
THE
WORD

WHAT'S THE WORD

DESIREE HARDWICK

WHAT'S THE WORD

iUniverse books may be ordered through booksellers or by contacting:

iUniverse
1663 Liberty Drive
Bloomington, IN 47403
www.iuniverse.com
844-349-9409

Because of the dynamic nature of the Internet, any web addresses or links contained in this book may have changed since publication and may no longer be valid. The views expressed in this work are solely those of the author and do not necessarily reflect the views of the publisher, and the publisher hereby disclaims any responsibility for them.

Any people depicted in stock imagery provided by Getty Images are models, and such images are being used for illustrative purposes only. Certain stock imagery © Getty Images.

ISBN: 978-1-6632-6182-3 (sc)
ISBN: 978-1-6632-6183-0 (e)

Library of Congress Control Number: 2024906767

Print information available on the last page.

iUniverse rev. date: 04/22/2024

CONTENTS

Old Testament vii

New Testament ix

Special Thanks xi

Glossary 89

BOOKS OF THE BIBLE

OLD TESTAMENT

Genesis

Exodus

Leviticus

Numbers

Deuteronomy

Joshua

Judges

Ruth

1 Samuel

2 Samuel

1 Kings

2 Kings

1 Chronicles

2 Chronicles

Ezra

Nehemiah

Esther

Job

Proverbs

Ecclesiastes

Song of Songs

Isaiah

Jeremiah

Lamentations

Ezekiel

Daniel

Hosea

Joel

Amos

Obadiah

Jonah

Micah

Nahum

Habakkuk

Zephaniah

Malachi

Psalm

BOOKS OF THE BIBLE

NEW TESTAMENT

Matthew	*2 Thessalonians*
Mark	*1 Timothy*
Luke	*2 Timothy*
John	*Titus*
Acts	*Philemon*
Romans	*Hebrews*
1 Corinthians	*James*
2 Corinthians	*1 Peter*
Galatians	*2 Peter*
Ephesians	*1 John*
Philippians	*2 John*
Colossians	*3 John*
1 Thessalonians	*Jude*

Revelations

SPECIAL THANKS

Dear God, thank you for your love, grace, and mercy. I come before you today with a heart full of gratitude, as you have continued to hear and answer my prayers, providing blessing after blessing. I thank you, Lord, for the good and in times of trials that have strengthened me. Oh Lord, I will continue to give you all the honor, glory, and praise. In Jesus' name, I give thanks. Amen

Proverbs 3:3-5

Trust in the Lord with all your heart, and do not lean on your own understanding. In all your ways acknowledge him, and he will make straight your paths.

To my husband, Nelson T. Hardwick Jr. - Thank you for your unwavering love, constant presence, and your caring spirit that has helped us through some of the most challenging times. I love and appreciate you more than words can express. God has blessed us with 20 years of marriage, and I look forward to all the blessings that the future holds for us.

To my wonderful sons, aka "my sweets", Nelson and Dyson. You are both amazing gifts from God, and I am so blessed and thankful for your unconditional love. You have been my motivation, and now, I am grateful that you've motivated me to pursue some of my dreams. Every day, I pray for you and want you always to remember that "I love you no matter what."

Special thanks to my son Dyson Hardwick
who designed the cover.
Family
We love because he first loved us.
1 John 4:19

This book is dedicated to my mother, Pearl L. Moore, who showed me that with trust and belief in God, all things are possible. She was a woman who survived and endured many things in her life, and the word of God saw her through. I am truly grateful for her love, guidance, and unwavering faith. I can still hear her singing her favorite song.

"We've Come This Far By Faith."

We have come this far by faith,
Leaning on the Lord,
Trusting in his holy word,
He's never failed me yet.
Singin' oh, oh, oh, can't turn around,
We've come this far by faith.
Just the other day, I heard a man say,
He didn't believe in God's word,
But I can truly say that I have found the way,
And he's never failed me yet.

Pearl L. Moore
June 11, 1933-May 15, 2006

WHAT'S
THE
WORD

DAY 1

Beginning

John 1:1 In the beginning was the Word, and the Word was with God, and the Word was God. Read Hebrews 1:10

_____

_____

_____

_____

DAY 2

Trust

Mark 11:24 Therefore I tell you, whatever you ask in prayer, believe that you have received it, and it will be yours. Read Proverbs 3:5

_____

_____

_____

_____

DAY 3

Strength

Isaiah 41:10 "So do not fear, for I am with you, do not be dismayed, for I am your God. I will strengthen you and help you, I will uphold you with my righteous hand." Read Philippians 4:13

_____

_____

_____

_____

DAY 4
Protection
2 Thessalonians 3:3 But the Lord is faithful. He will establish you and guard you against the evil one. Read Isaiah 54:17

_____

_____

_____

_____

DAY 5
Love
1 Corinthians 16:14 Do everything in love. Read Romans 13:8

_____

_____

_____

_____

DAY 6
Compassion
Colossians 3:12 Therefore, as Gods chosen people, holy and dearly loved, clothe yourselves with compassion, kindness, humility, gentleness, and patience. Read Colossians 3:12-13

_____

_____

_____

_____

DAY 7

Spirit

Proverbs 18:14 A man's spirit will endure sickness, but a crushed spirit who can bear? Read Romans 8:26

_____

_____

_____

_____

DAY 8

Peace

Romans 15:13 May the God of hope fill you with all joy and peace as you trust him, so that you may overflow with hope by the power of the Holy Spirit.
Read Psalm 34:14

_____

_____

_____

_____

DAY 9

Goals

2 Chronicles 15:7 "But as for you, be strong and do not give up, for your work will be rewarded." Read Philippians 3:14-16

_____

_____

_____

_____

DAY 10
Sin

James 4:17 Anyone, then, who knows the good he ought to do and doesn't do it, sins. Read Romans 3:23

_____

_____

_____

_____

DAY 11
Debt

Proverbs 22:7 The rich rule over the poor, and the borrower is the slave to the lender. Read Romans 13:8

_____

_____

_____

_____

DAY 12
Doubt

Hebrews 11:6 And without faith it is impossible to please God, because anyone who comes to him must believe that he exists and that he rewards those who earnestly seek him. Read Proverbs 3:5-8

_____

_____

_____

_____

DAY 13

Money

1 Timothy 6:10 For the love of money is a root of all kinds of evil. Some people, eager for money, have wandered from the faith and pierced themselves with many griefs. Read Proverbs 11:28

_____

_____

_____

_____

DAY 14

Trouble

Nahum 1:7 The Lord is good, a refuge in times of trouble. He cares for those who trust in him. Read Psalm 34:6

_____

_____

_____

_____

DAY 15

Encourage

1 Thessalonians 5:11 Therefore encourage one another and build each other up, just as in fact you are doing. Read 2 Timothy 1:7

_____

_____

_____

_____

DAY 16
Steadfast

Galatians 6:9 Let us not become weary of doing good, for at the proper time we will reap a harvest if we do not give up. Read James 1:12

_____

_____

_____

_____

DAY 17
Forgive

Ephesians 4:32 Be kind and compassionate to one another, forgiving each other, just as in Christ God forgave you. Read Matthew 6:14

_____

_____

_____

_____

DAY 18
Time

Ecclesiastes 3:1 To everything there is a season, and a time to every purpose under the heaven. Read Ecclesiastes 3:2-11

_____

_____

_____

_____

DAY 19

Talent

1 Peter 4:10 Each of you has been blessed with one of God's many wonderful gifts to be used in the service of others. So, use your gift well. Read 1 Corinthians 12:7-11

_____

_____

_____

_____

DAY 20

Commitment

Proverbs 16:3 Commit thy works unto the Lord, and thy thoughts shall be established. Read Psalm 37:5

_____

_____

_____

_____

DAY 21

Friendship

1 Thessalonians 5:11 Therefore encourage one another, and build one another up, just as you are doing. Read Proverbs 17:17

_____

_____

_____

_____

DAY 22

Sorrow

John 16:22 And ye now therefore have sorrow: but I will see you again, and your heart shall rejoice, and your joy no man taketh from you. Read 1 Peter 5:7

_____

_____

_____

_____

DAY 23

Abandonment

1 Timothy 5:8 People who don't take care of their relatives, and especially their own families, have given up their faith. They are worse than someone that doesn't have faith in the Lord. Read Psalm 27:10

_____

_____

_____

_____

DAY 24

Eyes

Matthew 6:22 The light of the body is the eye: if therefore thine eye be single, thy whole body shall be full of light. Read Psalm 118:23

_____

_____

_____

_____

DAY 25
Ears

Isaiah 30:21 Whether you turn to the right or to the left, your ears will hear a voice behind you, saying, "This is the road! Now follow it." Read Psalm 78:1

_____

_____

_____

_____

DAY 26
Hands

Nehemiah 6:9 For they made all of us afraid, saying, "their hands shall be weakened from the work, that it be not done. Now, therefore, O God strengthen my hands." Read Mark 10:16

_____

_____

_____

_____

DAY 27
Feet

Psalm 18:33 You make my feet run as fast as those deer, and you help me stand on the mountains. Read John 13:14

_____

_____

_____

_____

DAY 28

Heart

Ezekiel 36:26 "I will give you a new heart and put a new spirit in you. I will remove from you your heart of stone and give you a heart of flesh." Read Proverbs 3:5-6

_____

_____

DAY 29

Fasting

Matthew 6: 16-18 "When you fast, do not look somber as the hypocrites do, for they disfigure their faces to show men they are fasting. I tell you the truth, they have received their reward in full. But when you fast, put oil on your head and face, so that it will not be obvious to men that you are fasting, but only to your Father, who is unseen; and your Father, who sees what is done in secret, will reward you." Read Nehemiah 1:4

_____

_____

DAY 30

Faith

Hebrews 11:6 Without faith it is impossible to please God, because anyone who comes to him must believe that he exists and that he rewards those who earnestly seek him. Read Romans 10:17

_____

_____

_____

DAY 31

Wisdom

James 1:5 If any of you lacks wisdom, let him ask God, who gives generously to all without reproach, and it will be given him. Read Proverbs 2:1-22

_____

_____

_____

DAY 32

Discourage

Joshua 1:9 Have I not commanded you? "Be strong and courageous. Do not be frightened, and do not be dismayed, for the LORD your God is with you wherever you go." Read Psalm 31:24

_____

_____

_____

DAY 33

Healing

James 5:15 And the prayer of faith will save the one who is sick, and the Lord will raise him up. And if he has committed sins, he will be forgiven.
Read Psalm 147:3

_____

_____

_____

_____

DAY 34

Happiness

Isaiah 12:3 Therefore with joy shall ye draw water out of the wells of salvation. Read Proverbs 14:13

_____

_____

_____

_____

DAY 35

Sadness

1 Peter 5:10 And after you have suffered a little while, the God of all grace, who has called you to his eternal glory in Christ, will himself restore, confirm, strengthen, and establish you. Read Nehemiah 2:2-5

_____

_____

_____

_____

DAY 36

Success

Habakkuk 2:3 "At the time I have decided, my words will come true. You can trust what I say about the future. It may take a long time but keep waiting; it will happen." Read Psalm 20:4

_____

_____

_____

_____

DAY 37

Hunger

Luke 6:21 Blessed are you who hunger now, for you will be satisfied. Read John 6:35

_____

_____

_____

_____

DAY 38

Confusion

2 Corinthians 4:8 We are hard pressed on every side, but not crushed; perplexed, but not in despair. Read Galatians 1:6-9

_____

_____

_____

_____

DAY 39

Denial

Luke 9:23 And he said to all, "If anyone would come after me, let him deny himself and take up his cross daily and follow me." Read Matthew 10:33

_____

_____

_____

_____

DAY 40
Acknowledge
Jeremiah 9:6 "You live in the midst of deception; in their deceit they refuse to acknowledge me." Declares the Lord. Read Proverbs 3:6

_____

_____

_____

_____

DAY 41
Humility
Proverbs 22:4 The reward for humility and fear of the Lord is riches and honor and life. Read Philippians 2:3

_____

_____

_____

_____

DAY 42
.Image
Genesis 9:6 Whoever shed the blood, by man shall his blood be shed, for God made man in his own image. Read Colossians 1:15-16

_____

_____

_____

_____

DAY 43

Curse

Romans 12:14 Bless those who persecute you; bless and do not curse. Read Colossians 3:8

_____

_____

_____

_____

DAY 44

Slavery

1 Corinthians 7:21 Were you a slave when you were called? Don't let it trouble you-although if you gain your freedom do so. Read 1 Peter 2:16

_____

_____

_____

_____

DAY 45

Transgression

Isaiah 43:25 "I, even I, am he who blots out your transgressions, for my own sake, and remembers your sins no more." Read James 1:14

_____

_____

_____

_____

DAY 46

Omnipotent

Revelation 1:8 "I am the Alpha and the Omega," says the Lord God, "who is, and who was, and who is to come, the Almighty." Read Jeremiah 32:17

_____

_____

_____

_____

DAY 47

Leadership

Galatians 6:9 Let us not become weary in doing good, for at the proper time we will reap a harvest if we do not give up. Read Exodus 18:21

_____

_____

_____

_____

DAY 48

Gifts

1 Peter 4:10 As each has received a gift, use it to serve one another, as good stewards of God's varied grace: Read Ephesians 2:8-9

_____

_____

_____

_____

DAY 49

Dance

Jeremiah 31:13 "Then maidens will dance and be glad, young men and old as well, I will turn their mourning into gladness: I will give them comfort and joy instead of sorrow." Read Psalm 149:3

_____

_____

_____

_____

DAY 50

Music

1 Samuel 16:23 Whenever the spirit from God came upon Saul, David would take his harp and play. Then relief would come to Saul, he would feel better, and the evil spirit would leave him. Read James 5:13

_____

_____

_____

_____

DAY 51

Honor

1 Peter 2:17 Show proper respect to everyone. Love the brotherhood of believers, fear God, honor the King. Read Ephesians 6:1-4

_____

_____

_____

_____

DAY 52

Promise

2 Corinthians 1:20 For no matter how many promises God has made, they are "Yes" in Christ. And so through him the "Amen" is spoken by us to the glory of God. Read Acts 2:39

_____

_____

_____

DAY 53

Covet

Luke 12:15 "Watch out! Be on your guard against all kinds of greed; a man's life does not consist in the abundance of his possessions." Read Exodus 20:17

_____

_____

_____

DAY 54

Covenant

Deuteronomy 7:9 Know therefore that the Lord your God is God; he is the faithful God, keeping his covenant of love to a thousand generations of those who love him and keep his commands. Read Hebrews 13:20-21

_____

_____

_____

_____

DAY 55
Lazy
Proverbs 1:25 If you want too much and are too lazy to work, it could be fatal. Read Proverbs 13:4

_____

_____

_____

_____

DAY 56
Disobedient
Titus 3:10 Warn a divisive person once, and then a second time. After that, have nothing to do with him. You may be sure that such a man is warped and sinful; he is self-condemned. Read 2 Timothy 3:1-5

_____

_____

_____

_____

DAY 57
Obedience
Isaiah 1:19-20 "If you are willing and obedient, you will eat the best from the land; but if you resist and rebel, you will be devoured by the sword." For the mouth of the Lord has spoken. Read Ephesians 6:1

_____

_____

_____

DAY 58

Guidance

Psalm 32:8 I will instruct you and teach you in the way you should go; I will counsel you and watch over you. Read Proverbs 24:6

_____

_____

_____

_____

DAY 59

Crying

Revelation 21:4 "He will wipe away every tear from their eyes. There will be no more death or mourning or crying or pain, for the old order of things has passed away." Read Ecclesiastes 3:4.

_____

_____

_____

_____

DAY 60

Joy

1 Thessalonians 5:16-18 Be joyful always; pray continually; give thanks in all circumstances, for this is God's will for you in Jesus Christ. Read Galatians 5:22

_____

_____

_____

_____

DAY 61

Lonely

Isaiah 41:10 "Fear not, for I am with you; be not dismayed, for I am your God; I will strengthen you, I will help you, I will uphold you with my righteous right hand." Read Luke 5:22

_____

_____

_____

_____

DAY 62

Racism

John 7:24 "Stop judging by mere appearances, and make a right judgment." Read Romans 2:11

_____

_____

_____

_____

DAY 63

Rainbow

Genesis 9:13 "I have set my rainbow in the clouds, and it will be the sign of the covenant between me and the earth." Read Genesis 9:14-17

_____

_____

_____

_____

DAY 64

Clouds

Matthew 24:30 "Then will appear in heaven the sign of the Son of Man, and then all the tribes of the earth will mourn, and they will see the Son of Man coming on the clouds of heaven with power and great glory." Read Ecclesiastes 11:3-4

_____

_____

_____

_____

DAY 65

Sunrise

Mark 16:2 And very early on the first day of the week, when the sun had risen, they went to the tomb. Read Psalm 113:3

_____

_____

_____

_____

DAY 66

Stress

Proverbs 12:5 Anxiety in a man's heart weighs him down, but a good word makes him glad. Read Philippians 4:6

_____

_____

_____

_____

DAY 67

Repent

Acts 3:19-20 "Repent, then, and turn to God, so that your sins may be wiped out, that times of refreshing may come from the Lord; and that he may send the Christ, who has been appointed for you-even Jesus." Read 1 John 1:9

_____

_____

_____

DAY 68

Stubborn

Ephesians 4:18 They are darkened in their understanding, alienated from the life of God because of the ignorance that is in them, due to their hardness of heart.
Read Psalms 81:11-12

_____

_____

_____

DAY 69

Sickness

Romans 5:3-5 More than that, we rejoice in our sufferings, knowing that suffering produces endurance, and endurance produces character, and character produces hope that will never disappoint us. Read Jeremiah 33:6

_____

_____

_____

DAY 70

Flowers

Song of Songs 2:12 "Flowers appear on the earth; the season of singing has come; the cooing of doves is heard in our land." Read Isaiah 40:8

_____

_____

_____

_____

DAY 71

Mother

Proverbs 31:28-29 "Her children arise and call her blessed; her husband also, and he praises her: "Many women do noble things, but you surpass them all." Read 2 Kings 4:30

_____

_____

_____

_____

DAY 72

Father

Ephesians 6:4 Fathers, do not exasperate your children; instead bring them up in the training and instruction of the Lord. Read Psalm 103:13

_____

_____

_____

_____

DAY 73

Brothers

Galatians 6:1 Brothers, if someone is caught in a sin, you who are spiritual should restore him gently. But watch yourself, or you also may be tempted. Read James 1:19

DAY 74

Women

Titus 2:3-5 Older women likewise are to be reverent in behavior, not slanderers or slaves to much wine. They are to teach what is good, and so train the young women to love their husbands and children, to be self-controlled, pure, working at home, kind, and submissive to their own husbands, so that the word of God may not be reviled. Read Matthew 27:55-56

DAY 75

Stranger

Hebrews 13:1-2 Keep being concerned about each other as the Lord's followers should. Be sure to welcome strangers into your home. By doing this, some people have welcomed angels as guests, without even knowing it. Read Leviticus 19:33

DAY 76

Baby

Jeremiah 1:5 "Before I formed you in the womb I knew you, and before you were born, I consecrated you; I appointed you a prophet to the nations." Read 1 Samuel 1:27-28

_____

_____

_____

_____

DAY 77

Youth

1 Timothy 4:12 Don't let anyone make fun of you, just because you are young. Set an example for other followers by what you say and do, as well as by your love, in faith and in purity. Read Ecclesiastes 11:9-10

_____

_____

_____

DAY 78

Pain

Romans 8:18 For I consider that the sufferings of this present time are not worth comparing with the glory that is to be revealed to us. Read Job 14:22

_____

_____

_____

DAY 79

Travel

Proverbs 16:9 In his heart a man plans his course, but the Lord determines his steps. Read Numbers 10:29-32

_____

_____

_____

_____

DAY 80

Water

Ezekiel 36:25 "I will sprinkle clean water on you, and you shall be clean; I will cleanse you from all impurities and from all your idols.". Read John 4:13-14

_____

_____

_____

DAY 81

Famine

Amos 8:11-12 "Behold, the days are coming," declares the Lord God, "when I will send a famine on the land— not a famine of bread, nor a thirst for water, but of hearing the words of the Lord. Men will stagger from sea to sea and wander from north to east, searching for the word of the Lord, but they will not find it." Read Matthew 24:7

_____

_____

_____

DAY 82

Servant

Galatians 5:13 For you were called to freedom, brothers. Only do not use your freedom as an opportunity for the flesh, but through love serve one another. Read Mark 10:45

_____

_____

_____

_____

DAY 83

Service

Colossians 3:23-24 Whatever you do, work at it with all your heart, as working for the Lord, not for men, since you know that you will receive an inheritance from the Lord as a reward. Read James 2:18

_____

_____

_____

_____

DAY 84

Children

3 John 1:4 I have no greater joy than to hear my children are walking in the truth. Read Psalm 127:3

_____

_____

_____

DAY 85

Condemn

Luke 6:37 "Do not judge, and you will not be judged. Do not condemn and you will not be condemned. Forgive and you will be forgiven." Read John 3:17

DAY 86

Demons

1 Corinthians 10:21 You cannot drink the cup of the Lord and the cup of demons too; you cannot have a part in both the Lord's table and the table of the demons. Read 1 Peter 5:8

DAY 87

Freedom

Galatians 5:1 It is for freedom that Christ has set us free. Stand firm, then, and do not let yourselves be burdened again by the yoke of slavery. Read 2 Corinthians 3:17

DAY 88
Mankind
Psalm 8:4 What is man that you are mindful of him, and the son of man that you care for him? Read Jeremiah 32:27

_____

_____

_____

_____

DAY 89
Weary
Hebrews 12:3 Consider him who endured from sinners such hostility against himself, so that you may not grow weary or fainthearted. Read Isaiah 40:31

_____

_____

_____

_____

DAY 90
Wilderness
Ezekiel 34:25 "I will make with them a covenant of peace and banish wild beasts from the land, so that they may dwell securely in the wilderness and sleep in the woods." Read Deuteronomy 32:10

_____

_____

_____

_____

DAY 91
Plants
Genesis 1:11-12

And God said, "Let the earth sprout vegetation, plants yielding seed, and fruit trees bearing fruit in which is their seed, each according to its kind, on the earth." And it was so. The earth brought forth vegetation, plants yielding seed according to their own kinds, and trees bearing fruit in which is their seed, each according to its kind. And God saw that it was good. Read Matthew 15:13

_____

_____

_____

DAY 92
Fish
John 21:13 Jesus came and took the bread and gave it to them and did the same with the fish. Read Jonah 1:17

_____

_____

_____

DAY 93
Bread
John 6:35 Jesus said to them, "I am the bread of life; whoever comes to me shall not hunger, and whoever believes in me shall never thirst. Read Ruth 2:14-16

_____

_____

DAY 94

Wine

Ecclesiastes 9:7 Go, eat your bread with joy, and drink your wine with a merry heart, for God has already approved what you do. Read Joel 2:19

_____

_____

_____

_____

DAY 95

Drunkenness

Ephesians 5: 17-18 Therefore, do not be foolish, but understand what the Lord's will is. Do not get drunk on wine, which leads to debauchery, instead be filled with the spirit; Read Romans 13:13

_____

_____

_____

DAY 97

Eat

Luke 12:22-23 Then Jesus said to his disciples: "Therefore I tell you, do not worry about your life, what you will eat; or about your body, what you will wear. Life is more than food, and the body more than clothes." Read Genesis 9:3

_____

_____

_____

DAY 98

Trees

Revelation 22:14 God will bless all who have washed their robes. They will each have the right to eat fruit from the tree that gives life, and they can enter the gates of the city. Read Daniel 4:10-12

_____

_____

_____

DAY 99

Beauty

1 Peter 3:3-4 Do not let your adorning be external—the braiding of hair and the putting on of gold jewelry, or the clothing you wear— but let your adorning be the hidden person of the heart with the imperishable beauty of a gentle and quiet spirit, which in God's sight is very precious. Read Song of Songs 4:1-7

_____

_____

_____

DAY 100

Reward

Hebrews 11:6 And without faith it is impossible to please him, for whoever would draw near to God must believe that he exists and that he rewards those who seek him. Read Ephesians 6:8

_____

_____

_____

DAY 101

Unity

Romans 12:16 Live in harmony with one another. Do not be proud, but be willing to associate with people of low position. Do not be conceited. Read 1 Peter 3:8

_____

_____

_____

_____

DAY 102

Liturgy

Acts 2:42 They devoted themselves to the apostles' teaching and to the fellowship, to the breaking of bread and to prayer. Read James 5:16

_____

_____

_____

_____

DAY 103

Judgment

Deuteronomy 1:17 "Do not show partiality in judging; hear both small and great alike. Do not be afraid of any man, for judgment belongs to God. Bring me any case too hard for you, and I will hear it." Read Matthew 7:1-2

_____

_____

_____

DAY 104

Darkness

Micah 7:8 Do not gloat over me, my enemy! Though I have fallen, I will rise. Though I sit in darkness, the Lord is my light. Read 1 Samuel 2:9

_____

_____

_____

_____

DAY 105

Smell

Leviticus 2:2 And bring it to Aaron's sons the priests. And he shall take from it a handful of the fine flour and oil, with all its frankincense, and the priest shall burn this as its memorial portion on the altar, a food offering with a pleasing aroma to the Lord. Read Numbers 15:1-3

_____

_____

_____

DAY 106

Truth

Proverbs 12:22 The Lord detests lying lips, but he delights in men who are truthful. Read John 14:17

_____

_____

_____

DAY 107

Hasty

Ecclesiastes 5:2 Do not be quick with your mouth, do not be hasty in your heart to utter anything before God. God is in heaven and you are on earth, so let your words be few. Read Proverbs 21:5

_____

_____

_____

_____

DAY 108

Worry

Psalm 55:22 Our Lord, we belong to you. We tell you what worries us, and you won't let us fall. Read Joshua 1:9

_____

_____

_____

_____

DAY 109

Thankful

Ephesians 5:20 Always use the name of our Lord Jesus Christ to thank God the Father for everything. Read 1 Thessalonians 5:18

_____

_____

_____

_____

DAY 110

Good

Psalm 34:8 Taste and see that the Lord is good; blessed be the man who takes refuge in him. Read Romans 8:28

_____

_____

_____

_____

DAY 111

Follow

John 8:12 Again Jesus spoke to them, saying, "I am the light of the world. Whoever follows me will not walk in darkness but will have the light of life." Read John 12:26

_____

_____

_____

_____

DAY 112

Mountains

Isaiah 54:10 "Though the mountains be shaken and the hills be removed, yet my unfailing love for you will not be shaken nor my covenant of peace be removed," says the Lord who has compassion on you. Read Revelation 16:20

_____

_____

_____

DAY 113

Elders

James 5:14 Is anyone among you sick? Let him call for the elders of the church, and let them pray over him, anointing him with oil in the name of the Lord. Read Titus 1:5-9

_____

_____

_____

_____

DAY 114

Gambling

Hebrews 13:5 Keep your life free from love of money, and be content with what you have, for he has said, "I will never leave you nor forsake you." Read Mark 8:36

_____

_____

_____

DAY 115

Transformation

Romans 12:2 Do not be conformed to this world, but be transformed by the renewal of your mind, that by testing you may discern what is the will of God, what is good and acceptable and perfect. Read Acts 3:19

_____

_____

_____

DAY 116

Teaching

James 3:1 Not many of you should become teachers, my brothers, for you know that we who teach will be judged with greater strictness. Read 2 Timothy 3:16-17

_____

_____

_____

_____

DAY 117

Eternity

Revelation 1:18 "I am the Living One; I was dead, and behold I am alive for ever and ever! And I hold the keys of death and Hades." Read Daniel 4:34

_____

_____

_____

DAY 118

Confess

Hosea 14:1-2 Return, O Israel, to the Lord, your God. Your sins have been your downfall! Take the words with you and return to the Lord. Say to him: "Forgive all our sins and receive us graciously, that we may offer the fruit of our lips." Read 1 John 1:9

_____

_____

_____

DAY 119

Rivalry

Philippians 2:2-3 Complete my joy by being of the same mind, having the same love, being in full accord and of one mind. Do nothing from rivalry or conceit, but in humility count others more significant than yourselves. Read James 4:6

DAY 120

Division

Titus 3:9-11 But avoid foolish controversies, and genealogies, and arguments and quarrels about the law, because these are unprofitable and useless. Warn a divisive person once, and then warn him a second time. After that, have nothing to do with him. Read Romans 16:17-18

DAY 121

Glory

2 Peter 1:3 His divine power has granted to us all things that pertain to life and godliness, through the knowledge of him who called us to his own glory and excellence. Read 1 Corinthians 10:31

DAY 122

Strife

Proverbs 10:12 Hatred stirs up strife, but love covers all offenses.
Read Proverbs 17:14

_____

_____

_____

_____

DAY 123

Guilt

Romans 6:23 For the wages of sin is death, but the gift of God is
eternal life in Christ Jesus our Lord. Read 1 Peter 5:7

_____

_____

_____

_____

DAY 124

Submission

James 4:7 Submit yourselves, then to God. Resist the devil, and
he will flee from you. Read Hebrews 13:17

_____

_____

_____

_____

DAY 125

Tithe

Luke 6:38 "Give, and it will be given to you. A good measure, pressed down, shaken together and running over, will be poured into your lap. For with the measure you use, it will be measured to you." Read Malachi 3:10

_____

_____

_____

DAY 126

Refuge

John 10:10-11 "The thief comes only to steal and kill and destroy. I have come that they may have life and have it abundantly. I am the good shepherd. The good shepherd lays down his life for the sheep." Read Psalm 125:2-3

_____

_____

_____

DAY 127

Wounded

1 Peter 2:24 He himself bore our sins in his body on the tree, that we might die to sin and live for righteousness. By his wounds you have been healed. Read Jeremiah 30:17

_____

_____

_____

DAY 128

Mourning

Lamentations 3:31-33 For men are not cast off by the Lord forever. Though he brings grief, he will show compassion, so great is his unfailing love. For he does not willingly bring affliction or grief to the children of men. Read Matthew 5:4

_____

_____

_____

_____

DAY 129

Singing

1 Chronicles 16:9 Sing to him, sing praise to him; tell of all his wondrous acts. Read Zephaniah 3:17

_____

_____

_____

_____

DAY 130

Saints

Revelation 14:12 Here is a call for the endurance of the saints, those who keep the commandments of God and their faith in Jesus. Read Psalm 30:4

_____

_____

_____

DAY 131

Thanksgiving

Jonah 2:9 "But I, with a song of Thanksgiving, will sacrifice to you. What I have vowed I will make good. Salvation comes from the Lord." Read Thessalonians 1:3

_____

_____

_____

_____

DAY 132

Change

2 Corinthians 5:17 Therefore, if anyone is in Christ, he is a new creation; the old has gone, and the new has come! Read Psalm 51:10

_____

_____

_____

_____

DAY 133

Shackles

Isaiah 58:6 "Is not this the kind of fasting I have chosen: to loose the chains of injustice and untie the cords of the yoke, to set the oppressed free, and break every yoke?" Read Nahum 1:12-13

_____

_____

_____

_____

DAY 134
Brutality
Revelation 20:10 And the devil who had deceived them was thrown into the lake of fire and sulfur where the beast and the false prophet were, and they will be tormented day and night forever and ever. Read Luke 21:34-36

_____

_____

_____

_____

DAY 135
Mindfulness
Romans 12:2 Do not be conformed to this world, but be transformed by the renewal of your mind, that by testing you may discern what is the will of God, what is good and acceptable and perfect. Read Joshua 1:8

_____

_____

_____

DAY 136
Abuse
James 3:10 Out of the same mouth come praise and cursing. My brothers, this should not be. Read James 4:1-17

_____

_____

_____

DAY 137

Culture

2 Thessalonians 2:15 So then, brothers, stand firm and hold to the teachings we passed onto you, whether by word of mouth or by letter. Read Zacariah 2:11-13

_____

_____

_____

_____

DAY 138

Depression

Psalm 34: 17-18 When the righteous cry for help, the Lord hears and delivers them out of all their troubles. The Lord is near to the brokenhearted and saves the crushed in spirit. Read Isaiah 41:10

_____

_____

_____

_____

DAY 139

Procrastination

Proverbs 13:4 The soul of the sluggard craves and gets nothing, while the soul of the diligent is richly supplied. Read Ecclesiastes 11:4

_____

_____

_____

_____

DAY 140

Liberate

Zephaniah 3:12 "But I will leave in your midst a people humble and lowly. They shall seek refuge in the name of the Lord." Read Isaiah 2:4

_____

_____

_____

_____

DAY 141

Suicide

Ecclesiastes 7:17 Do not be over wicked, and do not be a fool-why die before your time. Read 1 Corinthians 3:16-17

_____

_____

_____

_____

DAY 142

Understanding

Psalm 119:34 Give me understanding, that I may keep your law and observe it with my whole heart. Read 2 Timothy 3:1-17

_____

_____

_____

_____

DAY 143

Anxiety

Matthew 6:34 Don't worry about tomorrow. It will take care of itself. You have enough to worry about today. Read Philippians 4:6-7

_____

_____

_____

DAY 144

Reconcile

2 Corinthians 5:18 God has done it all! He sent Christ to make peace between himself and us, and he has given us the work of making peace between himself and others. Read Ephesians 4:32

_____

_____

_____

DAY 145

Wickedness

Mark 7:20-23 And he said, "What comes out of a person is what defiles him. For from within, out of the heart of man, come evil thoughts, sexual immorality, theft, murder, adultery, coveting, wickedness, deceit, sensuality, envy, slander, pride, foolishness. All these evil things come from within, and they defile a person." Read Ezekiel 18:19-24

_____

_____

_____

DAY 146

Structure

1 Corinthians 14:40 But everything should be done in a fitting and orderly way. Read Ephesians 5:15-17

DAY 147

Rest

Genesis 2:3 And God blessed the seventh day and made it holy, because on it he rested from all the work of creating that he had done. Read Deuteronomy 5:12-14

DAY 148

Angels

Judges 13:6 Then the woman came and told her husband, "A man of God came to me, and his appearance was like the appearance of the angel of God, very awesome. I did not ask him where he was from, and he did not tell me his name." Read Mark 8:38

DAY 149

Approach

Jeremiah 29:13 You will seek me and find me when you seek me with all your heart. Read 1 John 5:14

_____

_____

_____

_____

DAY 150

Bravery

Deuteronomy 31:6 "Be strong and courageous. Do not fear or be in dread of them, for it is the Lord your God who goes with you. He will not leave you or forsake you." Read 2 Timothy 1:7

_____

_____

_____

_____

DAY 151

Bold

Acts 28:31 Proclaiming the kingdom of God and teaching about the Lord Jesus Christ with all boldness and without hindrance. Read Proverbs 28:1

_____

_____

_____

_____

DAY 152

Rock

1 Samuel 2:2 "There is no one holy like the Lord; there is no one besides you; there is no Rock like our God." Read Psalm 62:6

_____

_____

_____

DAY 153

Gold

Ezekiel 28:4-5 By your wisdom and understanding you have gained wealth for yourself, and amassed gold and silver into your treasuries. By your great skill in trading you have increased your wealth, and because of your wealth your heart has grown proud. Read Haggai 2:7-9

_____

_____

_____

DAY 154

Silver

Exodus 20:22-23 Then the Lord said to Moses, "Tell the Israelites this; You have seen for yourselves that I have spoken to you from heaven: Do not make any gods to be alongside me; do not make for yourselves gods of silver or gold." Read Zachariah 13:9

_____

_____

_____

DAY 155

Favor

Psalm 90:17 Let the favor of the Lord our God be upon us: and prosper for us the work of our hands- O prosper the work of our hands! Read Genesis 18:3

_____

_____

_____

_____

DAY 156

Dependence

Isaiah 41:13 For I, the Lord your God, hold your right hand; it is I who say to you," Do not fear, I will help you." Read Exodus 14:14

_____

_____

_____

_____

DAY 157

Control

Proverbs 25:28 Like a city whose walls are broken down is a man who lacks self-control. Read 2 Timothy 1:7

_____

_____

_____

_____

DAY 158

Witness

Isaiah 43:10 "You are my witnesses," declares the Lord, "and my servant whom I have chosen, that you may know and believe me and understand that I am he. Before me no god was formed, nor shall there be any after me." Read Mark 16:15-16

_____

_____

_____

DAY 159

Rebellious

Nehemiah 9:17 They refused to listen and failed to remember the miracles you performed among them. They became stiff-necked and, in their rebellion, appointed a leader in order to return to their slavery. But you are a forgiving God, gracious and compassionate, slow to anger and abounding in love. Therefore, you did not desert them. Read 2 Thessalonians 2:3

_____

_____

DAY 160

Beloved

Colossians 3:12 As God's chosen ones, holy and beloved, clothe yourselves with compassion, kindness, humility, meekness, and patience. Read 1 John 4:7-8

_____

_____

DAY 161

Praise

Hebrews 13:15 Through Jesus, therefore, let us continually offer to God a sacrifice of praise-the fruit of lips that confess his name. Read Daniel 2:23

_____

_____

_____

DAY 162

Deceit

Jeremiah 17:9 The heart is deceitful above all things, and desperately sick; who can understand it? Read Ephesians 5:6-7

_____

_____

_____

DAY 163

Blasphemy

James 3:7-10 All kinds of animals, birds, reptiles, and sea creatures are being tamed and have been tamed by mankind, but no human being can tame the tongue. It is a restless evil, full of deadly poison. With the tongue we praise our Lord and Father, and with it we curse human beings, who have been made in God's likeness. Out of the same mouth come praise and cursing. My brothers and sisters, this should not be. Read Leviticus 24:10-16

_____

_____

_____

DAY 164

Meditate

Joshua 1:8 "Do not let this Book of the Law depart from your mouth; but meditate on it day and night, so that you may be careful to do everything written in it. Then you will be prosperous, and successful." Read Matthew 6:6

_____

_____

_____

_____

DAY 165

Dreams

Numbers 12:6 And he said, "Hear my words: When there are prophets among you, I the Lord make myself known to them in visions; I speak to them in dreams. Read Daniel 1:17

_____

_____

_____

DAY 166

Scripture

2 Timothy 3:16 All scripture is inspired by God and is useful for teaching, for reproof, for correction, and for training in righteousness. Read Romans 15:4

_____

_____

_____

DAY 167

Wise

Ephesians 5:15-16 Be very careful, then how you live-not as unwise but as wise, making the most of every opportunity because the days are evil.

Read Proverbs 10:1

_____

_____

_____

DAY 168

Jealousy

Zephaniah 1:18 Neither their silver nor their gold will be able to save them on the day of the Lord's wrath. In the fire of his jealousy the whole world will be consumed, for he will make a sudden end of all who live on earth. Read 1 Corinthians 3:3

_____

_____

_____

DAY 169

Worthy

Matthew 6:26 Look at the birds of the air: they neither sow nor reap nor gather into barns, and yet your heavenly Father feeds them. Are you not of more value than they? Read Philippians 4:8-9

_____

_____

_____

DAY 170

False

1 John 4:10 Beloved, do not believe every spirit, but test the spirits to see whether they are from God: for many false prophets have gone out into the world.
Read 2 Peter 2:2

_____

_____

_____

DAY 171

Respect

Esther 1:20 Then when the king's edict is proclaimed throughout all his vast realm, "all the women will respect their husbands, from the least to the greatest."
Read Romans 13:7

_____

_____

_____

DAY 172

Serpent

1 Peter 5:8 Be sober-minded; be watchful. Your adversary the devil prowls around like a roaring lion, seeking someone to devour. Read Genesis 3:1

_____

_____

_____

DAY 173

Healer

James 5:16 Therefore, confess your sins to one another and pray for one another, that you may be healed. The prayer of a righteous person has great power as it is working. Read Mark 9:24-27

DAY 174

Fire

Deuteronomy 4:24 For the Lord your God is a consuming fire, a jealous God. Read Jeremiah 23:29

DAY 175

Competition

1 Corinthians 9:24 Do you not know that in a race all the runners run, but only one receives the prize? So run that you may obtain it. Read 2 Timothy 2:5

DAY 176

Renewal

Titus 3:5-6 He saved us, not because of works done by us in righteousness, but according to his own mercy, by the washing of regeneration and renewal of the Holy Spirit, whom he poured out on us generously through Jesus Christ our Savior. Read Psalm 51:10

DAY 177

Harvest

Galatians 6:9 Let us not become weary in doing good, for at the proper time we will reap a harvest if we do not give up. Read Deuteronomy 24:19

DAY 178

Hostility

Ephesians 4:31 "Let all bitterness and wrath and anger and clamor and slander be put away from you, along with all malice." Read James 4:1

DAY 179

Idols

Habakkuk 2:18 "What profit is an idol when its maker has shaped it, a metal image, a teacher of lies? For its maker trusts in his own creation when he makes speechless idols!" Read Jonah 2:8

_____

_____

_____

_____

DAY 180

Idle

2 Thessalonians 3:11 We hear that some among you are idle. They are not busy; they are busybodies. Read Ecclesiastes 10:18

_____

_____

_____

_____

DAY 181

Justice

Micah 6:8 He has told you, O man, what is good; and what does the LORD require of you but to do justice, and to love kindness, and to walk humbly with your God? Read Hosea 12:6

_____

_____

_____

_____

DAY 182

Journey

Judges 18:5-6 Then they said to him," Please inquire of God to learn whether our journey will be successful." The priest answered them, "Go in peace. Your journey has the Lord's approval." Read Psalm 23:4

_____

_____

_____

_____

DAY 183

King

Isaiah 33:22 For the Lord is our judge, the Lord is our lawgiver, the Lord is our King; it is he who will save us. Read Daniel 4:37

_____

_____

_____

_____

DAY 184

War

Matthew 24:6 "You will hear of wars and rumors of wars, but see to it that you are not alarmed. Such things must happen, but the end is still to come." Read Ephesians 6:17

_____

_____

_____

DAY 185

Storms

Mark 4:39 And he awoke and rebuked the wind and said to the sea, "Peace! Be still!" And the wind ceased, and there was a great calm. Read Nahum 1:3

_____

_____

_____

_____

DAY 186

Blindness

2 Corinthians 4:4 The god of this age has blinded the minds of unbelievers, so that they cannot see the light of the *gospel* of the glory of Christ who is the image of God. Read Luke 6:39

_____

_____

_____

_____

DAY 187

Careless

Matthew 12:36 "But I tell you that men will have to give account on the day of judgment for every careless word they have spoken." Read 2 Timothy 2:16

_____

_____

_____

DAY 188

Blood

Hebrews 9:22 In fact, the law requires that nearly everything be cleansed with blood, and without shedding of blood there is no forgiveness. Read 1 John 1:7

_____

_____

_____

_____

DAY 189

Tribulation

Matthew 24:21" For then there will be great distress, unequaled from the beginning of the world until now-and never to be equaled again." Read Revelation 7:14

_____

_____

_____

_____

DAY 190

Prayer

1 Thessalonians 5:16-18 Be joyful always; pray continually; give thanks in all circumstances, for this is God's will for you in Christ Jesus. Read Mark 11:24

_____

_____

_____

DAY 191

Sword

1 Samuel 17:47 "All those gathered here will know that it is not by the sword or spear that the Lord saves; for the battle is the Lord's, and he will give all of you into our hands." Read Ephesians 6:17

_____

_____

_____

DAY 192

Man

Job 14:1-5 "Man who is born of a woman is of few days and full of trouble. He comes out like a flower and withers; he flees like a shadow and continues not. And do you open your eyes on such a one and bring me into judgment with you? Who can bring a clean thing out of an unclean? There is not one. Since his days are determined, and the number of his months is with you, and you have appointed his limits that he cannot pass." Read Ruth 2:20

_____

_____

_____

DAY 193

Son

Proverbs 1:8 Listen, my son, to your father's instruction and do not forsake your mother's teaching. Read 1 John 5:11

_____

_____

_____

DAY 194

Significance

1 Corinthians 6:19-20 Do you not know that your body is a temple of the Holy Spirit, who is in you, whom you have received from God? You are not your own; you were bought at a price. Therefore, honor God with your body. Read Philippians 2:2-5

DAY 195

Everlasting

Daniel 7:14 "He was given authority, glory and sovereign power; all peoples, nations and men of every language worshiped him His dominion is an everlasting dominion that will not pass away, and his kingdom is one that will never be destroyed." Read Nehemiah 9:5

DAY 196

Birth

1 Samuel 1:27-28 "For this child I prayed, and the LORD has granted me my petition that I made to him. So now I give him to the Lord. For his whole life he will be given over to the Lord." And he worshipped the Lord there. Read John 3:3

DAY 197

Borrower

Proverbs 22:7 The rich rule over the poor, and the borrower is servant to the lender. Read Romans 13:8

_____

_____

_____

_____

DAY 198

Noble

Isaiah 32:8 But the noble man makes noble plans, and by noble deeds he stands. Read Ruth 3:11

_____

_____

_____

_____

DAY 199

Kindness

Titus 3:4 But when the kindness and love of God our Savior appeared, he saved us, not because of righteous things we had done, but because of his mercy. Read Zechariah 7:9

_____

_____

_____

_____

DAY 200

Courage

Joshua 1:9 "Have I not commanded you? Be strong and courageous. Do be terrified; do not be discouraged, for the Lord your God will be with you wherever you go." Read Ephesians 6:10-11

DAY 201

Warrior

Jeremiah 20:11 But the Lord is with me like a mighty warrior: so my persecutors will stumble and not prevail. They will fail and be thoroughly disgraced; their dishonor will never be forgotten. Read Ephesians 6:10-18

DAY 202

Animals

Leviticus 11:46-47 'These are the regulations concerning animals, birds, every living thing that moves about in the water and every creature that moves along the ground. You must distinguish between the unclean and the clean, between living creatures that may be eaten and those that may not be eaten." Read Genesis 1:21

DAY 203

Living

Colossians 3:1-4 If then you were raised with Christ, seek those things which are above, where Christ is, sitting at the right hand of God. Set your mind on things above, not on things on the earth. For you died, and your life is hidden with Christ in God. When Christ who is our life appears, then you also will appear with Him in glory. Read Romans 12:1

DAY 204

Grace

Philemon 1:25 The grace of the Lord Jesus Christ be with your spirit. Read 1 Corinthians 15:10

DAY 205

Flesh

Galatians 5:16-18 I say then: Walk in the Spirit, and you shall not fulfill the lust of the flesh. For the flesh lusts against the Spirit, and the Spirit against the flesh; and these are contrary to one another, so that you do not do the things that you wish. But if you are led by the Spirit, you are not under the law. Read Luke 24:36-40

_____

_____

_____

_____

DAY 206

Struggle

James 1:2-4 Count it all joy, my brothers, when you meet trials of various kinds, for you know that the testing of your faith produces steadfastness. And let steadfastness have its full effect, that you may be perfect and complete, lacking in nothing.
Read Hebrews 12:3-6

_____

_____

_____

_____

DAY 207
Isolation
Proverbs 18:1 Whoever isolates himself seeks his own desire; he breaks out against all sound judgment. Read Ecclesiastes 4:9-10

_____

_____

_____

_____

DAY 208
Silence
Lamentations 3:25-26 The Lord is good to those whose hope is in him; it is good to wait quietly for the salvation of the Lord. Read Habakkuk 2:20

_____

_____

_____

_____

DAY 209
Light
Ecclesiastes 11:7 Light is sweet, and it pleases the eyes to see the sun. Read Micah 7:8

_____

_____

_____

_____

DAY 210

Family

1 Timothy 5:8 But if anyone does not provide for his own, and especially for those of his household, he has denied the faith and is worse than an unbeliever. Read Esther 9:26-28

_____

_____

_____

_____

DAY 211

Neighbor

Galatians 5 :14-15 The entire law is summed up in a single command: "Love your neighbor as yourself." If you keep on biting and devouring each other, watch out or you will be destroyed by each other. Read Leviticus 19:18

_____

_____

_____

DAY 212

Salvation

Isaiah 12:2 "Surely God is my salvation; I will trust and not be afraid. The Lord, the Lord, is my strength and my song; he has become my salvation." Read Acts 2:38

_____

_____

_____

DAY 213

Emotions

James 1:20 For the anger of man does not produce the righteousness of God. Read Proverbs 15:18

_____

_____

_____

_____

DAY 214

Prepare

John 14:2-3 "In my Father's house are many rooms; if it were not so, I would have told you. I am going there to prepare a place for you. And if I go and prepare a place for you, I will come back and take you with me that you also may be where I am." Read Zephaniah 1:7

_____

_____

_____

_____

DAY 215

Godless

2 Timothy 2:16 "Avoid godless chatter, because those who indulge in it will become more ungodly. Read Jude 1:4-5

_____

_____

_____

_____

DAY 216

Authority

Romans 13:1 Let every soul be subject to the governing authorities. For there is no authority except from God, and the authorities that exist are appointed by God. Read Hebrews 13:17

_____

_____

_____

_____

DAY 217

Value

Proverbs 10:2 Ill-gotten treasures have no lasting value, but righteousness delivers from death. Read 1 Samuel 26:24

_____

_____

_____

_____

DAY 218

Riches

1 Timothy 6:17 Command those who are rich in this present world not to be arrogant nor to put their hope in wealth, which is so uncertain, but to put their hope in God, who richly provides us with everything for our enjoyment. Read Matthew 6:24

_____

_____

_____

DAY 219
Thanks
1 Thessalonians 5:16-18 Be joyful always; pray continually; give thanks in all circumstances, for this is God's will for you in Christ Jesus. Read Nehemiah 12:40

_____

_____

_____

_____

DAY 220
Violence
Genesis 6:11 Now the earth was corrupt in God's sight and was full of violence. Read Matthew 11:12

_____

_____

_____

_____

DAY 221
Build
Jude 1:20-21 But you dear friends, build yourselves up in the most holy faith and pray in the Holy Spirit. Keep yourselves in God's love as you wait for the mercy of our Lord Jesus Christ to bring you eternal life. Read Romans 15:1-2

_____

_____

_____

DAY 222
Dwell
Isaiah 43:18-19 "Forget the former things; do not dwell on the past. See, I am doing a new thing! Now it springs up; do you not perceive it? I am making a way in the desert and streams in the wasteland." Read Psalm 133:1-3

_____

_____

_____

_____

DAY 223
Marriage
Hebrews 13:4 Marriage should be honored by all, and the marriage bed kept pure, for God will judge the adulterer and all the sexually immoral. Read Matthew 1:25

_____

_____

_____

DAY 224
Divorce
Matthew 19:8 Jesus replied, "Moses permitted you to divorce your wives because your hearts were hard. But it was not this way from the beginning." Read 1 Corinthians 7:10-11

_____

_____

_____

DAY 225

Grumbling

Philippians 2:14-16 Do everything without grumbling or arguing, so that you may become blameless and pure, children of God without fail in a crooked and depraved generation, in which you shine like stars in the universe as you hold out the word of life-in order that I may boast on the day of Christ that I did not run or labor for nothing.

Read Lamentations 3:39

_____

_____

_____

_____

DAY 226

Excellent

Philippians 4:8-9 Finally brothers, whatever is true, whatever is noble, whatever is right, whatever is pure, whatever is lovely, whatever is admirable-if anything is excellent or praiseworthy-think about such things. Whatever you have learned or received or heard from me or seen in me-put it into practice. And the God of peace will be with you.

Read Psalm 8:1

_____

_____

_____

_____

DAY 227

Cruel

Obadiah 1:10-11 You were cruel to your relatives the descendants of Jacob. Now you will be destroyed, disgraced forever. On the day you stood aloof while strangers carried off his wealth and foreigners entered his gates and cast lots for Jerusalem, you were like one of them. Read Proverbs 11:17

_____

_____

_____

_____

DAY 228

Disaster

Daniel 9:13-14 Just as it is written in the Law of Moses, all this disaster has come on us, yet we have not sought the favor of the LORD our God by turning from our sins and giving attention to your truth. The LORD did not hesitate to bring the disaster on us, for the LORD our God is righteous in everything he does; yet we have not obeyed him.
Read Isaiah 3:11

_____

_____

_____

_____

DAY 229

Healthy

Luke 11:34 "Your eye is the lamp of your body. When your eyes are good, your whole body also is full of light. But when they are unhealthy your body also is full of darkness." Read 3 John 1:2

_____

_____

_____

_____

DAY 230

Preaching

1 Corinthians 15:1-5 Now, brothers, I want to remind you of the gospel I preached to you, which you received and on which you have taken your stand. By this gospel you are saved, if you hold firmly to the word I preached to you. Otherwise, you have believed in vain. For what I received I passed on to you as of first importance; that Christ died for our sins according to the Scriptures, and that he appeared to Peter and then to the twelve. Read Exodus 4:10-12

_____

_____

_____

_____

DAY 231

Obey

Joshua 24:24 And the people said unto Joshua, The Lord our God will we serve, and his voice will we obey. Read Deuteronomy 30:8

_____

_____

_____

_____

DAY 232

Nurture

Deuteronomy 6:6-7 These commandments that I give you today shall be upon your hearts. Impress them om your children. Talk about them when you sit at home, and when you walk along the road, when you lie down, and when you get up. Read Ephesians 4:15

_____

_____

_____

_____

DAY 233

Naked

Job1:21 "Naked I came from my mother's womb, and naked I will depart. The Lord gave and the has taken away; may the name of the Lord be praised." Read Ezekiel 16:7-8

_____

_____

_____

DAY 234

Lightning

Exodus 20:18-20 When the people saw the thunder and lightning and heard the trumpet and saw the mountain in smoke, they trembled with fear. They stayed at the distance and said to Moses, "Speak to us yourself and we will listen. But do not have God speak to us or we will die." Moses said to the people, "Do not be afraid. God has come to test you, so that the fear of God will be with you to keep you from sinning." Read Psalm 77:18

_____

_____

_____

_____

DAY 235

Hypocrite

Matthew 7:1-5 "Do not judge, or you too will be judged.

For in the same way you judge others, you will be judged, and with the measure you use, it will be measured to you." "Why do you look at the speck of sawdust in your brother's eye and pay no attention to the plank in your own eye? How can you say to your brother, 'Let me take the speck out of your eye,' when all the time there is a plank in your own eye? You hypocrite, first take the plank out of your own eye, and then you will see clearly to remove the speck from your brother's eye. Read 1 John 4:20

_____

_____

_____

_____

DAY 236

Army

Joel 2:11 The Lord thunders at the head of his army; his forces are beyond number, and mighty are those who obey his command. The day of the Lord is great; it is dreadful. Who can endure it? Read 1 King 20:28

_____

_____

_____

_____

DAY 237

Comfort

2 Corinthians 1:3-5 Praise God, the Father of our Lord Jesus Christ! The Father is a merciful God, who always gives us comfort. He comforts us when we are in trouble, so that we can share that same comfort with others in trouble. We share in the terrible sufferings of Christ, but also in the wonderful comfort he gives. Read 1 Thessalonians 2:10-12

_____

_____

_____

_____

DAY 238

Exile

Ezekiel 39:28-29 "Then they will know that I am the Lord their God, for though I sent them into exile among the nations, I will gather them to their own land, not leaving any behind. I will no longer hide my face from them, for I will pour out my Spirit on the house of Israel, declares the Sovereign Lord."
Read 1 Peter 2:9-11

_____

_____

_____

_____

DAY 239

Quiet

Ecclesiastes 9:16-18 So I said, "Wisdom is better than strength." But the poor man's wisdom is despised, and his words are no longer heeded. The quiet words of the wise are more to be heeded than the shouts of a ruler of fools. Read Lamentations 3:26

_____

_____

_____

_____

DAY 240

Temple

1 Corinthians 6:19-20 Do you not know that your body is a temple of the Holy Spirit, who is in you, whom you have received from God? You are not your own; you were bought at a price. Therefore, honor God with your body. Read John 2:18-22

_____

_____

_____

_____

DAY 241

Suffering

Romans 5:2-5 Christ has also introduced us to God's undeserved kindness on which we take our stand. So we are happy, as we look forward to sharing in the glory of God. But that's not all! We gladly suffer because we know that suffering helps us endure. And endurance builds character, which gives us hope that will never disappoint us. All of this happens because God has given us the Holy Spirit, who fills our hearts with love. Read 1 Peter 5:10

_____

_____

_____

_____

DAY 242

Prophesy

Acts 2:17 "In the last days, God says, I will pour out my Spirit on all people. Your sons and daughters will prophesy, your young men will see visions, your old men will dream dreams." Read Luke 21:25-27

_____

_____

_____

_____

DAY 243

Mature

Philippians 3:15-16 All of us who are mature should take such a view of things, And if on some point you think differently, that too God will make clear to you. Only let us live up to what we have already attained. Read Ephesians 4:13-15

_____

_____

_____

DAY 244

Walk

Leviticus 26:12 I will walk among you and be your God, and you will be my people. Read Micah 4:2-5

_____

_____

_____

DAY 245

Reveal

Luke 10:22 "All things have been committed to me by my Father. No one knows who the Son is except the Father, and no one knows who the Father is except the Son and those to whom the Son chooses to reveal him." Read Numbers 12:6

_____

_____

_____

DAY 246

Oppression

Ecclesiastes 4:1-2 Again I looked and saw all the oppression that was taking place under the sun: I saw the tears of the oppressed- and they have no comforter; power was on the side of their oppressors- and they have no comforter. And I declared that the dead, who had already died, are happier than the living. Read Psalm 9:9

_____

_____

_____

DAY 247

Prepared

2 Timothy 4:2 Preach the Word; be prepared in season and out of season; correct, rebuke, and encourage-with great patience and careful instruction. Read Revelation 21:1-4

_____

_____

DAY 248

Interpretation

Daniel 2:30 "As you were lying there, O king your mind turned to things to come, and the revealer of mysteries showed you what is going to happen. As for me, this mystery has been revealed to me, not because I have greater wisdom than other living men, but so that you, O king may know the interpretation and that you may understand what went through your mind." Read 2 Peter 1:19-21

_____

_____

_____

_____

DAY 249

Uphold

Isaiah 41:10 Fear not, for I am with you; be not dismayed, for I am your God; I will strengthen you, I will help you, I will uphold you with my righteous right hand. Read 1 Samuel 24:15

_____

_____

_____

_____

DAY 250

Victory

1 John 5:1-5 Everyone who believes that Jesus is the Christ is born of God, and everyone who loves the father loves his child as well. This is how we know that we love the children of God: by loving God and carrying out his commands. This is love for God: to keep his commands. And his commands are not burdensome, for everyone born of God overcomes the world. This is the victory that has overcome the world, even our faith. Who is it that overcomes the world? Only the one who believes that Jesus is the Son of God. Read Deuteronomy 20:4

_____

_____

_____

_____

GLOSSARY

1.	Beginning	John 1:1, Hebrews 1:10
2.	Trust	Mark 11:24, Proverbs 3:5
3.	Strength	Isaiah 41:10, Philippians 4:13
4.	Protection	2 Thessalonians 3:3, Isaiah 54:17
5.	Love	1 Corinthians 16:14, Romans 13:8
6.	Compassion	Colossians 3:12, Colossians 3:12-13
7.	Spirit	Proverbs 18:14, Romans 8:26
8.	Peace	Romans 15:13, Psalm 34:14
9.	Goals	2 Chronicles 15:7, Philippians 31:14-16
10.	Sin	James 4:17, Romans 3:23
11.	Debt	Proverbs 22:7, Romans 13:8
12.	Doubt	Hebrews 11:6, Proverbs 3:5-8
13.	Money	1 Timothy 6:10, Proverbs 11:28
14.	Trouble	Nahum 1:7, Psalm 34:6
15.	Encourage	1 Thessalonians 5:11, 2 Timothy 1:7
16.	Steadfast	Galatians 6:9, James 1:12
17.	Forgive	Ephesians 4:32, Matthew 6:4
18.	Time	Ecclesiastes 3:1, Ecclesiastes 3:2-11
19.	Talent	1 Peter 4:10, 1 Corinthians 12:7-11
20.	Commitment	Proverbs 16:3, Psalm 37:5
21.	Friendship	1 Thessalonians 5:11, Proverbs 17:17
22.	Sorrow	John 16:22, 1 Peter 5:7
23.	Abandon	1 Timothy 5:8, Psalm 27:10
24.	Eyes	Matthew 6:22, Psalm 118:23
25.	Ears	Isaiah 30:21, Psalms 78:1
26.	Hands	Nehemiah 6:9, Mark 10:16
27.	Feet	Psalm 18:33, John 13:14
28.	Heart	Ezekiel 36:26, Proverbs 3:5-6

29.	Fasting	Matthew 6:16-18, Nehemiah 1:4
30.	Faith	Hebrews 11:6, Romans 10:17
31.	Wisdom	James 1:5. Proverbs 2:1-22
32.	Discourage	Joshua 1:9, Psalm 31:24
33.	Healing	James 5:15, Psalm 147:3
34.	Happiness	Isaiah 12:3, Proverbs 14:13
35.	Sadness	1 Peter 5:10, Nehemiah 2:2-5
36.	Success	Habakkuk 2:3, Psalm 20:4
37.	Hunger	Luke 6:21, John 6:35
38.	Confusion	2 Corinthians 4:8, Galatians 1:6-9
39.	Denial	Luke 9:23, Matthew 10:33
40.	Acknowledge	Jeremiah 9:6 Proverbs 3:6,
41.	Humility	Proverbs 22:4, James 4:6
42.	Image	Genesis 9:6, Galatians 3:28
43.	Curse	Romans 12:14, Colossians 3:8
44.	Slavery	1 Corinthians 7:21, 1 Peter 2:16
45.	Transgression	Isaiah 43:25, James 1:14
46.	Omnipotent	Revelation 1:8, Jeremiah 32:17
47.	Leadership	Galatians 6:9, Exodus 18:21
48.	Gifts	1 Peter 4:10, Ephesians 2:8-9
49.	Dance	Psalm 149:3, Jeremiah 31:13
50.	Music	Samuel 16:23, James 5:13
51.	Honor	1 Peter 2:17, Ephesians 6:1-4
52.	Promise	2 Corinthians 1:20, Acts 2:39
53.	Covet	Luke 12:15, Exodus 20:17
54.	Covenant	Deuteronomy 7:9, Hebrews 3:20-21
55.	Lazy	Proverbs 21:25-26, Proverbs 13:4
56.	Disobedient	Titus 3:10, 2 Timothy 3:1-5
57.	Obedience	Isaiah 1:19, Ephesians 6:1
58.	Guidance	Psalm 32:8, Proverbs 24:6
59.	Crying	Revelation 21:4, Ecclesiastes 3:4

60.	Joy	1 Thessalonians 5:16-18, Galatians 5:22
61.	Lonely	Isaiah 41:10, Luke 5:16
62.	Racism	John 7:24, Romans 2:11
63.	Rainbow	Genesis 9:13, Genesis 9:14-17
64.	Clouds	Matthew 24:30, Ecclesiastes 11:3-4
65.	Sunrise	Mark 16:2, Psalm 113:3
66.	Stress	Proverbs 12:25, Philippians 4:6
67.	Repent	Acts 3:19, 1 John 1:9
68.	Stubborn	Ephesians 4:18, Psalm 81:11-12
69.	Sickness	Romans 5:3-4, Exodus 23:25
70.	Flowers	Song of Songs 2:12, Isaiah 40:8
71.	Mother	Proverbs 31:28-29, 2 Kings 4:30
72.	Father	Ephesians 6:4, Psalm 103:13
73.	Brother	Galatians 6:1, James 1:19
74.	Women	Titus 2:3-5, Matthew 27:55-56
75.	Stranger	Hebrews 13:1-2, Leviticus 19:33
76.	Baby	Jeremiah 1:5, 1 Samuel 1:27-28
77.	Youth	1 Timothy 4:12, Ecclesiastes 11:9-10
78.	Pain	Romans 8:18, Job 14:22
79.	Travel	Proverbs 16:9, Numbers 10:29-32
80.	Water	Ezekiel 36:25, John 4:13-14
81.	Famine	Amos 8:11, Matthew 24:7
82.	Servant	Galatians 5:13, Mark 10:45
83.	Service	Colossians 3:23-24, James 2:18
84.	Children	3 John 1:4, Psalm 127:3
85.	Condemn	Luke 6:37, John 3:17
86.	Demons	1 Corinthians 10:21, 1 Peter 5:8-9
87.	Freedom	Galatians 5:1, 2 Corinthians 3:17
88.	Mankind	Psalm 8:4, Jeremiah 32:27
89.	Weary	Hebrews 12:3, Isaiah 40:31
90.	Wilderness	Ezekiel 34:25, Deuteronomy 32:10

91.	Plants	Genesis 1 11:12, Matthew 15:13
92.	Fish	John 21:13, Jonah 1:17
93.	Bread	John 6:35, Read Ruth 2:14-16
94.	Fruit	Galatians 5:22-23, John 15:5
95.	Wine	Ecclesiastes 9:7, Joel 2:19
96.	Drunkenness	Ephesians 5:17-18, Romans 13:13
97.	Eat	Luke 12:22-23, Genesis 9:3
98.	Trees	Revelation 22:14, Daniel 4:10-12
99.	Beauty	1 Peter 3:3-4, Song of Songs 4:1-7
100.	Reward	Hebrews 11:6, Ephesians 6:8
101.	Unity	Romans 12:6, 1 Peter 3:8
102.	Liturgy	Acts 2:42, James 5:16
103.	Judgement	Deuteronomy 1:17, Matthew 7:1-2
104.	Darkness	Micah 7:8, 1 Samuel 2:9
105.	Smell	Leviticus 2:2, Ezekiel 20:41
106.	Truth	Proverbs 12:22, John 14:17
107.	Hasty	Ecclesiastes 5:2, Proverbs 21:5
108.	Worry	Psalm 55:22, Joshua 1:9
109.	Thankful	Ephesians 5:20, 1 Thessalonians 5:18
110.	Good	Psalm 34:8, Romans 8:28
111.	Follow	John 8:12, John 12:26
112.	Mountains	Isaiah 54:10, Revelation16:20
113.	Elders	James 5:14, Titus 1:6-9
114.	Gambling	Hebrew 13:5, Mark 8:36
115.	Transformation	Romans 12:2, Acts 3:19
116.	Teaching	James 3:1, 2 Timothy 3:16-17
117.	Eternity	Revelation 1:18, Daniel 3:4
118.	Confess	Hosea 14:1-2, 1 John 1:9
119.	Rivalry	Philippians 2:2-3, James 4:6
120.	Division	Titus 3:9-11, Romans 16:17-18
121.	Glory	2 Peter 1:3, 1 Corinthians 10.31

122.	Strife	Proverbs 10:12, Proverbs 17:14
123.	Guilt	Romans 6:23, 1 Peter 5:7
124.	Submission	James 4:17, Hebrews 13:17
125.	Tithe	Luke 6:28, Malachi 3:10
126.	Refuge	John 10:10, Psalm 125:2-3
127.	Wounded	1 Peter 2:24, Jeremiah 30:17
128.	Mourning	Lamentations 3:31-33, Matthew 5:4
129.	Singing	1 Chronicles 16:9, Zephaniah 3:17
130.	Saints	Revelation 14:12-13, Psalm 30:4
131.	Thanksgiving	Jonah 2:9, 2 Thessalonians 1:3
132.	Change	2 Corinthians 5:17, Psalm 51:10
133.	Shackles	Isaiah 58:6, Nahum 1:12-13
134.	Brutality	Revelation 20:10, Luke 21:34-36
135.	Mindfulness	Romans 12:2, Joshua 1:8
136.	Abuse	James 3:10, James 4:1-17
137.	Culture	2 Thessalonians 2:15, Zacariah 2:11-13
138.	Depression	Psalm 34:17-18, Isaiah 41:10
139.	Procrastination	Proverbs 13:4, Ecclesiastes 11:4
140.	Liberate	Zephaniah 3:12, Isaiah 2:4
141.	Suicide	Ecclesiastes 7:17, 1 Corinthians 3:16-17
142.	Understanding	Psalm 119:34, 2 Timothy 3:1-17
143.	Anxiety	Matthew 6:34, Philippians 4:6-7
144.	Reconcile	2 Corinthians 5:18, Ephesians 4:32
145.	Wickedness	Mark 7:20-23, Ezekiel 18:19-24
146.	Structure	1 Corinthians 14:40, Exodus 25:8
147.	Rest	Genesis 2:3, Deuteronomy 5:12-14
148.	Angels	Judges 13:6, Mark 8:38
149.	Approach	Jeremiah 29:12-13, 1 John 5:14
150.	Bravery	Deuteronomy 31:6, 2 Timothy 1-7
151.	Bold	Acts 28:31, Proverbs 28:1
152.	Rock	1 Samuel 2:2, Psalm 62:6

153.	Gold	Ezekiel 28:4, Haggi 2:7-9
154.	Silver	Exodus 20:20-23, Zachariah 13:9
155.	Favor	Psalm 90:17, Genesis 18:3
156.	Dependence	Isaiah 41:3, Exodus 14:14
157.	Control	Proverbs 25:28, 2 Timothy 1:7
158.	Witnessing	Isaiah 43:10, Mark 16:15-16
159.	Rebellious	Nehemiah 9:17. 2 Thessalonians 2:3
160.	Beloved	Colossians 3:12, 1 John 4:7-8
161.	Praise	Hebrews 13:15, Daniel 2:23
162.	Deceit	Jeremiah 17:9, Ephesians 5:6-7
163.	Blasphemy	James 3:7-10, Leviticus 24:10-16
164.	Mediate	Joshua 1:8, Matthew 6:6
165.	Dreams	Numbers 12:6, Daniel 1:17
166.	Scripture	2 Tomothy 3:16, Romans 15:4
167.	Wise	Ephesians 5:15, Proverbs 10:1
168.	Jealousy	Zephaniah 1:18, 1 Corinthians 3:3
169.	Worthy	Matthew 6:26, Philippians 4:8-9
170.	False	1 John 4:10, 2 Peter 2:2
171.	Respect	Ester 1:20, Romans 13:7
172.	Serpent	1 Peter 5:8, Genesis 3:1
173.	Healer	James 5:16, Mark 9:24-27
174.	Fire	Deuteronomy 4:24, Jeremiah 23:29
175.	Competition	1 Corinthians 9:24, 2 Timothy 2:5
176.	Renewal	Titus 3:5-6, Psalm 51:10
177.	Harvest	Galatians 6:9, Hosea 10:12
178.	Hostility	Ephesians 4:31, James 4:1
179.	Idols	Habakkuk 2:18, Jonah 2:8
180.	Idle	2 Thessalonians 3:11, Ecclesiastes 10:18
181.	Justice	Micah 6:8, Hosea 6:12
182.	Journey	Judges 18:5-6, Psalm 23:4
183.	King	Isaiah 33:22, Daniel 4:37

184.	War	Matthew 24:6, Ephesians 6:17
185.	Storms	Mark 4:39, Nahum 1:3
186.	Blindness	2 Corinthians 4:4, Luke 6:39
187.	Careless	Matthew 12:6, 2 Timothy 2:16
188.	Blood	Hebrews 9:22, 1 John 1:7
189.	Tribulation	Matthew 24:21, Revelation7:14
190.	Prayer	1 Thessalonians 5:16-18, Mark 11:24
191.	Sword	1 Samuel 17:47, Ephesian 6:17
192.	Man	Job 14:1-5, Ruth 2:20
193.	Son	Proverbs 1:8, 1 John 5:11
194.	Significance	1 Corinthians 6:19-20, Philippians 2:2-5
195.	Everlasting	Daniel 7:14, Nehemiah 9:5
196.	Birth	1 Samuel 1:27-28, John 3:3
197.	Borrower	Proverbs 22:7, Romans 13:8
198.	Noble	Isaiah 32:8, Ruth 3:11
199.	Kindness	Titus 3:4, Zachariah 7:9
200.	Courage	Joshua 1:9, Ephesians 6:10-11
201.	Warrior	Jeremiah 20:11, Ephesians 6:10-18
202.	Animals	Leviticus 11 :46-47, Genesis 1:21
203.	Living	Colossians 3:1-4, Romans 12:1
204.	Grace	Philemon 11:25, 1 Corinthians 15:10
205.	Flesh	Galatians 5:16-18, Luke 24:36-40
206.	Struggle	James 1:2-4, Hebrews 12:3-6
207.	Isolation	Proverbs 18:1 Ecclesiastes 4:9-10
208.	Silence	Lamentations 3:25-26, Habakkuk 2:20
209.	Light	Ecclesiastes 11:7, Micah 7:8
210.	Family	1 Timothy 5:8, Esther 9:26-28
211.	Neighbor	Galatians 5:14-15, Leviticus 19:18
212.	Salvation	Isaiah 12:2, Acts 2:38
213.	Emotions	James 1:20, Proverbs 15:18
214.	Prepare	John 14:2-3, Zephaniah 1:7

215.	Godless	2 Timothy 2:16, Jude 1:4-5
216.	Authority	Romans 13:1, Hebrew 13:17
217.	Value	Proverbs 10:2, 1 Samuel 26:24
218.	Riches	1 Timothy 6:17, Matthew 6:24
219.	Thanks	1 Thessalonians 5:16-18, Nehemiah 12:40
220.	Violence	Genesis 6:11, Matthew 11:12
221.	Build	Jude 1:20-21, Romans 15:1-2
222.	Dwell	Isaiah 43:18-19, Psalm 133:1-3
223.	Marriage	Hebrews 13:4, Matthew 1:25
224.	Divorce	Matthew 19:8, 1 Corinthians 7:10-11
225.	Grumbling	Philippians 2:14-16, Lamentations 3:39
226.	Excellent	Philippians 4:8-9, Psalm 8:1
227.	Cruel	Obadiah 1:10-11, Proverbs 11:17
228.	Disaster	Daniel 9:13-14, Isaiah 3:11
229.	Healthy	Luke 11:34, 3 John 1:2
230.	Preaching	1 Corinthians 15:1-5 Exodus 4:10-12
231.	Obey	Joshua 24:24, Deuteronomy 30:8
232.	Nurture	Deuteronomy 6:6-7, Ephesians 4:15
233.	Naked	Job 1:21, Ezekiel 16:7-8
234.	Lightning	Exodus 20:18-20, Psalm 77:18
235.	Hypocrite	Matthew 7:1-5, 1 John 4:20
236.	Army	Joel 2:11, 1 King 20:28
237.	Comfort	2 Corinthians 1 :3-5, 1 Thessalonians 2:10-12
238.	Exile	Ezekiel 39:28-29, 1 Peter 2:9-11
239.	Quiet	Ecclesiastes 9:16-18, Lamentations 3:26
240.	Temple	1 Corinthians 6:19-20, John 2:18-22
241.	Suffering	Romans 5:2-5, 1 Peter 5:10
242.	Prophesy	Acts 2:17, Luke 21:25-27
243.	Mature	Philippians 3:15-16, Ephesians 4:13-15
244.	Walk	Leviticus 26:12, Micah 4:2-5
245.	Reveal	Luke 10:22, Numbers 12:6

246. Oppression   Ecclesiastes 4:1-2, Psalm 9:9
247. Prepared   2 Timothy 4:2, Revelation 21:1-4
248. Interpretation Daniel 2:30, 2 Peter 1:19-21
249. Uphold   Isaiah 41:10, 1 Samuel 24:15
250. Victory   1 John 5:1-5, Deuteronomy 20:4

Printed in the United States
by Baker & Taylor Publisher Services